What is a Thought?

(A Thought is a Lot)

By

Jack Pransky and Amy Kahofer

Illustrated by T.M. DuSablon

SocialThinking.com

Social Thinking Publishing
San Jose, California

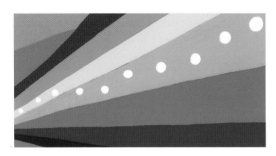

What is a Thought? (A Thought is a Lot)

Jack Pransky and Amy Kahofer
Illustrations by T.M. DuSablon

Library of Congress Number: 2011942275

ISBN: 978-1-936943-03-6
092015

Think Social Publishing, Inc.
3031 Tisch Way, Suite 800
San Jose, CA 95128
Tel: (877) 464-9278
Fax: (408) 557-8595

This book was printed and bound in Tennessee by Mighty Color Printing

Books can be ordered online at www.socialthinking.com

Reader Praise for *What is a Thought?*

"What is a Thought? is a beautiful and very powerful concept book which while simply put, evokes the complexity of how thoughts and feelings are intertwined. The text and teacher's guide will serve as a springboard for a wide range of discussions with children of varying ages and grades. The authors have crafted lessons aligned with Michelle Garcia Winner's Social Thinking model that are easily adapted for children with social learning challenges. This is an important book that will be read and enjoyed over and over, and raises new ideas and teachings each time."

–Debbie Meringolo, MA, MS, Special Educator

"This book is a godsend for young children and their teachers and parents. The principles explaining the inside out nature of life presented by Jack and Amy really do change young children's and adults' lives forever. Natural health, resilience, and wisdom are simply ignited. I have seen it first hand in my community based work for more than two decades. At last there is a beautiful children's book that supports this critical life changing learning."

–Kathy Marshall Emerson, Executive Director,
National Resilience Resource Center, University of Minnesota

"I have been using a draft of *What is a Thought* in my multi-age first/second grade class for years to introduce children to the idea that they have thoughts, to understand what thoughts are, and how those thoughts have the power to change. The verse and pictures in this book are simple, beautiful, and so appealing to children. They love the bright colors and the human images and the words stay with them long after they have heard the story. It's a book we read and reread every year and never tire of it."

–AHM, primary school teacher, Waterbury Vermont

"As we teach children to regulate their behavior by considering the thoughts and feelings of others, we must start by helping them understand how their own thoughts work. This book is a wonderful way to teach students to be aware of their thoughts and show them that they have the ability to choose how they react to their thoughts. This awareness and understanding of one's own thoughts is the first step in changing behavior."

–Ginny Thompson, MS-CCC, SLP &
Kristan Shimpi, Ph.D., founders of Teach Social First

"This gorgeously illustrated story is exactly what every early childhood educator and clinician needs – a way to explain the unexplainable: thoughts lead to feelings! The original artwork and winning rhyme are perfect for engaging children in reflective discussions on the abstract concept of a thought. An outstanding book with stimulating lesson plans that my staff and I will use with all our clients with language, learning, and social cognitive challenges."

–Nancy Tarshis MA, MS CCC-SLP
Supervisor of Speech and Language Services at the Children's
Evaluation and Rehabilitation Center at Einstein College of Medicine.

"I'm working with my second graders with *What is a Thought?* in my music classroom and am amazed to learn there are children who do not think they have thoughts! I don't know what Divine Wisdom will send to me, but one way or another, I am presenting your book to my students in a musical experience!"

–D. Van Hise, Elementary Music Teacher, North Plainfield, NJ

"My 9-year-old niece, Laci, couldn't wait to tell me that she got to the top of the climbing wall because she remembered what she learned in your book, **What is a Thought** ... that it was just her thoughts keeping her from reaching the top!"

–Lori Carpenos LMFT, West Hartford, CT

"I absolutely loved your book **What is a Thought? (A Thought is a Lot)**! I loved the simplicity and yet the power that lies underneath the words. When I heard the book read on the radio, I was moved. It is an amazing book written for kids, but one adults could benefit from tremendously for themselves."

–Sunil "Sunny" Punjabi, Teacher, Hong Kong

"I have been promoting **What is a Thought** to all my Supercoach academy friends and everyone is super-enthusiastic about it! What an amazing tool! Thanks to you both for this gift to the world."

–Veronique Pivetta, Three Principles Coach, Belgium

"**What is a Thought?** provides a simple but empowering message for both children and adults. The idea that a thought is powerful and that our thoughts create our feelings is simply and clearly explained. The illustrations support the text beautifully and create lots of opportunity for positive discussion. Each time I read this story, I am reminded of, and feel empowered by, 'the power of thought.'"

–Carol Balint, Special Educator, Hamilton, Ontario Canada

Dedication

To Dave, Jaime, Amanda, and Cory

Acknowledgements

To Syd Banks, for his inspiration

Introduction

*W*hat Is a Thought? introduces children to the amazing, creative power within us all, called thought. It is not a book about changing thoughts or changing behaviors, but rather a story to help children (and adults!) see how their own thinking creates their lives, moment to moment, day to day.

We have witnessed the amazing power this idea holds, in our own lives and in the lives of hundreds of people with whom we have worked. And, we believe sharing this message is important – from an early age – because it can lead to healthier choices and behaviors at any age.

What Is a Thought? gives children new hope that they can rise above whatever situation they may feel "stuck" in. It teaches that their thinking creates their feelings, as opposed to their feelings coming from the circumstances of their lives. Thoughts are awesome!

Stunning original artwork enhances this simple, yet profound message. Older children can read the book on their own; younger children can have an adult read it to them. A study guide is provided for teachers and parents, complete with an art glossary, lesson plans, experiential activities, handouts, and questions that explore the content more deeply and help teach the abstract concept of thought in child-friendly ways. Additional information is provided for teachers who work with children with social learning challenges, although all teachers will find the material useful in helping kids of all abilities.

We all have the power to change our lives for the better.

It starts with a thought.

What is a thought? A thought is a LOT!

What is a thought?

A thought is a lot,
A lot more than we think.

What does that mean?
Come have a look!

Thoughts have power!
Power for what?

Power to move you,
Power to fight,
Power to be peaceful,
With all of your might.

Power to love,
Power to hold,
Power to do
Whatever you're told.

Or not …

Power to be scared,
Power to be sad,
Power to be happy,
Power to be mad.

Power to have friends,
Power to make noise,
Power to be quiet,
Or play with your toys.

Yes, thoughts are behind
All of that stuff…
Because without having
a thought,
We couldn't do much!

Thoughts only have power,
If we follow their lead,
But how do we decide
Which thoughts to believe?

When our bodies feel calm,
Quiet and cool,
When we believe those thoughts,
We can trust them to rule.

When we are angry or sad,
Or just full of fear,
Our thoughts might
be saying stuff
We'd rather not hear.

This is the time
To let them pass through,
And not give them power
To tell us what to do.

If we're angry
at a friend
Who wasn't being fair,
Maybe he pushed in line,
Or she just didn't share.

We may think we want to
push our friend away,
Or grab that toy back for
ourselves to play.

But pushing and grabbing
Are just thoughts in our head.

What if something else
Could be thought of instead?

If we listen to thoughts   We won't get into trouble.
That come from deep inside,   We won't do any harm.
Thoughts that don't harm,   We will only be feeling
Thoughts that are wise,   The power of calm.

We always decide

Which thoughts we will feed,

Which thoughts to let go of,

Which thoughts to believe.

There are lots of things
That can give us a fright,
Like monsters hiding
Under our bed at night.

But when monsters and creatures
Come out of the blue,
The secret to know is,
They're just made-up thoughts, too!

Thoughts create our feelings,
But sometimes we don't know,
Why we feel the way we do,
Or why our mood is low.

Time passes by,
Our mood changes too,
And what once looked so real,
May no longer seem true.

When we're in a bad mood,
Calm nowhere in sight,
The thoughts in our mind
Will not come out right …
And might cause a fight!

So, if you're ready
to punch someone,
Or your tummy
is tied in knots,

Remember!
The only thing that
can get you
Are your own thoughts!

What is a thought?
Now I know!

A thought is a voice
Inside my head,
Telling a story
With words unsaid.

Looking at the world,
Making up what I see,
A thought is a gift…
Inside of me!

So now that we know
A lot about thought,
Our lives can be even better,
Believe it or not!

About the Authors

Amy Kahofer received her Master's degree in Special Education from the University of Vermont. She has been working with young children for more than 20 years as a special educator, preschool and kindergarten teacher, and currently is a first-grade teacher in a public school in Vermont.

Jack Pransky, Ph.D., has worked in the field of prevention since 1968 in a variety of capacities and now provides consultation, coaching, training, and counseling nationally and internationally. He has published many books for adults, including *Parenting from the Heart, Modello: A Story of Hope for the Inner City and Beyond, Prevention from the Inside-Out, Somebody Should Have Told Us!,* and also a curriculum for middle-school students called *Healthy Thinking/Feeling/Doing from the Inside Out.*

Amy and Jack live along a river in Moretown, Vermont.

About the Illustrator

Tina DuSablon began drawing long ago, while sitting at the kitchen table listening to her grandmother describe her self-taught illustration techniques. She has continued to draw and paint, alongside getting married, raising three boys, and working directly with children with special needs in Vermont public schools. She also lives in Moretown, VT.

Connecting Art to Real Life

The art in this book is abstract. It echoes the story line and whispers meaning, but only to readers who can interpret it. Younger children as well as many students with social learning challenges struggle to make these more abstract connections.

To help young readers better understand the story, we have included an art glossary, with a short description of the meaning the artist intended in each picture. Additional teaching tips, lessons, and activities are also provided to carry the discussion further and into deeper realms with older students. All adults will benefit from reading through this section; it offers questions that can be posed to readers of all ages to stimulate discussion on the concept of thought in a fun and engaging way.

As you read the story aloud, encourage children to guess what is going on in each picture. Explore different parts of the image and what each may convey (for instance, the setting, the question mark, the lightning bolt, the monster in the thought bubble, etc.). What emotions is the boy feeling? What is he thinking? By doing so, you encourage children to have thoughts of their own, and experience how powerful our thoughts can be.

Page i

We all have lots of thoughts in our head, little thoughts and big thoughts, thoughts that help us and thoughts that hinder us. We make up our own thoughts – they come from within.

Page 2

Sometimes our thoughts are BIG questions. This little guy has a big question about thought. He wants to understand what thought is, where it comes from, and why it is so important.

Page 4

Our thoughts come fast – like lightning! Sometimes our thoughts are just in our head, and sometimes they feel like they come from some other place deep inside, like from love.

Page 6

We make up our own thoughts and they are powerful! Sometimes they are the same as others' thoughts and sometimes they are different. This little boy is thinking about his toy surfboard.

Page 8

Just like riding a wave or soaking up the sun, our thinking can make us feel good. Our best ideas and decisions come from that kind of thinking, when we feel calm and cool.

Page 10

A prism reflects many different colors, just as our thoughts reflect many different feelings and behaviors. Through our thinking we can see situations from many different angles. We don't have to react based on impulse, but can step back and take another look.

Page 12

We are in charge of believing our thoughts... or not! Our thoughts can always change to help us feel cool, clear, and calm.

Page 14

Our thoughts can stay with us for a long, long time, or they can pass right by and pop! they disappear, just like a bubble.

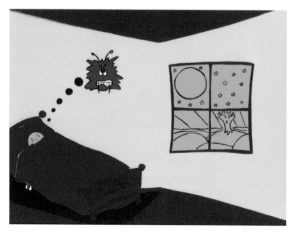

Page 16

Our thoughts are so powerful! Sometimes they can cause us to be really afraid, but if we realize we make up our thoughts, we know there are other possibilities. Then scary things might not seem so real, or so frightening!

Page 18

Thought can change. We don't have the same thoughts day after day. One day we think of monsters under the bed and the next day our thought shifts to something happy, like this scene. Our moods can help us tell if our thinking is unwise or not.

Page 20

The boy in the red shirt took the other boy's toy. At times we may not like what is happening. We can stop for a moment and decide if we really want to believe our thinking and act out those negative feelings... or not! Our best decisions come from thoughts that feel good.

Page 22

The thought bubbles are all wrapped in bows because thoughts are gifts. They come from inside, and we decide which thoughts to empower.

Page 24

Knowing about thought can really help us feel happier and our lives be better. We create our experience of life from moment to moment through our very own thinking!

Foreword to Lesson Plans and Activities
by Michelle Garcia Winner

What Is a Thought? is a charming children's book with a two-fold purpose. First, it is an engaging story that introduces to the audience the concept of thought and the amazing power our thoughts have on our lives. As a read-aloud book it is perfect for parents to read with their children at home, and is a valuable and important book for all early elementary school teachers to share in their general education classes.

Second, the Lesson Plans and Activities section of the book (found on the accompanying CD) transforms a simple children's story into a teaching tool that explores perspective taking, abstract/inferential language, and introduces abstract visual images to its readers. Many of today's students, especially those with autism spectrum disorders and nonverbal learning disorders which include social learning/social thinking challenges, struggle with interpreting language and communication that is abstract in nature. In varying degrees, these students lag behind their neurotypical peers for whom this type of social learning develops without direct teaching.

Whether we are parents or teachers, of typical or a-typical children, we strive to guide our children as they grow and develop. Before we can fully support emerging, resistant, or weak social communicators, it is important to understand where communication originates: from our own creative power of thought! This guide contains numerous lesson plans and activities to stimulate discussion within the classroom or at home about thought and its extraordinary influence in our lives. These lessons will help *all* children or students – whether or not they have a learning disability – understand the authors' key points, that:

* thoughts are amazingly powerful; we have the creative power to think anything
* our thinking creates our feelings and our behavior, not the other way around
* when our minds are calm we have access to natural wisdom and healthy feelings
* when we are riled up, angry, anxious, or in a bad mood, it is unwise to believe, trust or follow our thinking
* the extent to which we rely on wise thinking will determine how much we are guided by it

- our thinking has the power to change, and therefore our experience of things can change.

After reading through the book with children once or twice, teachers or parents may want to go back through it more slowly, using these proposed lessons to be sure readers grasp the various concepts. Each lesson has several components: the main point(s) to convey (located beneath each picture); a suggested lesson plan, with ideas to share with students as well as direct questions to ask, discussion points, and helpful notes to teachers/parents, including pointers when working with children with social thinking challenges. Adults are encouraged to create their own lessons to supplement or replace any here if doing so will better illustrate a particular point or make the activity more appealing to a particular reader.

The authors offer the following six questions as starting points for both adults and children to consider before and after reading this book.

- Where do thoughts come from?
- Do thoughts have power? If so, how?
- Can thoughts change? If so, how?
- Does everyone have the same thoughts? What about when the same event happens?
- Which comes first: thoughts or feelings?

- Do the thoughts we have in our heads have an effect on other people? If so, how?

What is a Thought? is relevant for all learners alike, and can be understood and appreciated on different levels. In working with children, we always begin with the thought that they are more capable than we adults often assume. That said, discussion about thought may be difficult for some students and easier for others. Our goal is to then teach to their individual needs.

Neurotypical children are born with an intact social thinking brain that learns and evolves as they grow. Children with social learning challenges can struggle in understanding that people can and do have different thoughts about the same thing and about each other. These children may also struggle with identifying emotions in themselves or others.

For students such as these, it is helpful to provide direct teaching of social learning concepts such as joint attention, social referencing, initiation of communication, abstract thinking, indirect language, as well as learning to see the world "though someone else's eyes." These and other Social Thinking® concepts are explained in detail, and helpful lesson plans provided, in the many books and workbooks published by Social Thinking Publishing.

Helpful information can also be found at www.socialthinking.com.

Thought is not something concrete children can hold in their hands, like a cup or a ball or an ice cream cone. Many of the activities in this guide ask children to use their imaginations to understand what is being described. Again, some children who process language in very literal ways and come into this world with brains that think in concrete, rather than abstract ways, may find it difficult to work through these activities, and may need some pre-teaching or expanded teaching before being able to make sense of the exercise. I've contributed a few sidebars directed to teachers of children with social learning challenges with additional helpful information.

For these reasons, when using the book in a therapeutic setting, we suggest that these lessons and activities are best suited for children who are on the higher functioning end of the social learning spectrum. Their functioning profile includes verbal communication, the ability to pretend and imagine, and at least a basic understanding that people have different thoughts from one another.

Four of the 10 Lesson Plans follow; find all 10 Lessons plus Activities and Handouts on the accompanying CD.

Lesson 1. Page 2.

The Power of Thought

Thought is so powerful we can create anything in our minds.

Anything we create comes from the power of thought.

What is a thought? The big question mark in the sky in the illustration on page 2 suggests this little guy has a big question about *thought* and wants to understand what thought is, where it comes from, and why it is so important. Sometimes we have little questions about things, and other times we have BIG questions.

Some questions to discuss with students:

- *Can we see thoughts?*
- *Can we touch thoughts?*
- *Can we smell thoughts?*
- *Can we taste thoughts?*
- *Can we hear thoughts with our ears?*

Note: This last question is a little tricky and is meant to provoke discussion. We can hear our own thoughts in our minds, but not with our ears. We cannot hear other people's thoughts, unless they speak them.

Instruct students to close their eyes and think about a star. Then imagine holding a star. Ask:

- *Can you do it?*
- *What did it feel like when you were thinking about it?*

Have students draw a picture of themselves holding a star.

Discussion

We can think anything! Just by thinking about something, like holding a star, you were able to create a picture, even though you didn't really hold a star in your hands. Thought helps us imagine things in our mind. Isn't it amazing that you were able to use your power of thought to make a beautiful picture? Thought is the most powerful gift we have.

Lessons 1-4 are included in the book as a sample; find all 10 Lessons and their accompanying Handouts on the enclosed CD.

Lesson 2. Pages 4, 6.

Thought Creates Feelings

Thoughts are so powerful they can give us good, bad, happy, sad, or mad feelings.

Our thoughts create our feelings!

The illustrations on these two pages show the power of thought and how it is lightning fast! Thoughts are what make us move or jump or run around (or stay still), but we don't realize we're thinking these thoughts. They happen so fast our bodies just follow our thoughts. Our thoughts create the way we feel, too, and sometimes it feels like the feelings come out of our heart, rather than from the thoughts in our brain. They too go by so fast we aren't even aware we're thinking them. Why do we feel the way we do, such as happy or sad or scared or mad? The reason is because we have happy or sad or scared or mad thoughts.

Activity. **The Feeling Parachute** (appropriate for grades K-1)

Materials:

Large parachute or large sheet/blanket

Instructions:

- Children and the teacher sit in a large circle with the parachute spread out in the center.
- Explain that all of the children sitting around the parachute are thoughts and the parachute is a feeling. "So we're all going to be the thinkers and we're going to move the parachute in a way that shows how different kinds of thinking makes us feel, okay?"
- The teacher chooses a child and asks the child to think about something that makes him or her feel a certain way. For example: "Josh, how does thinking about candy make you feel?" Josh may respond, "Excited!"

- Using the parachute, all the children and the teacher together move it up and down quickly to represent the feeling of being excited.
- Continue the activity a few more times, exploring different thoughts: calm, a lost toy, a birthday party, etc. Move the parachute according to feelings: be creative, and emphasize that our thoughts come before our feelings.
- Continue to reinforce the idea that our thinking is responsible for how we feel and act, just like it is responsible for the parachute moving the way it does.

Sidebar to the Teacher

Someone might bring up that pain happens independent of thought. We like this type of comment, it means kids are thinking! But how do we know we're in pain if we first do not have the thought of it? Almost everyone has had the experience of being deeply engaged in action and getting cut or bruised and not even noticing it until later. Then it hurts!

Children who struggle with social learning may not yet understand that people can have different thoughts about the same thing. They assume everyone has all the same thoughts! To better describe the various levels of social thinking and perspective taking that children with social learning challenges exhibit, Michelle Garcia Winner and her team developed the Social Thinking-Social Communication Profile, a six category assessment tool which can be helpful for teachers. Some children, who function at the lower levels of perspective taking may find concepts introduced in this book too difficult to understand. Learn more about the ST-SCP at www.socialthinking.com.

Activity. **Thought Creates Feelings** (appropriate for grades 2-5)

Materials (optional): Handout from CD, "Thought Creates Feelings." Children write or draw their answers instead of using verbal language during the activity.

Instructions:

* Divide students into pairs
* Ask the pairs of students a series of questions, such as:
  * *Think of something that makes you feel really happy.*
  * *Think of something that makes you feel sad.*
  * *Think of something that makes you feel angry.*
  * *Think of something that makes you feel scared.*
  * *Think of something that makes you feel excited.*
* Instruct students to tell their partner what they were thinking.

* When all questions have been asked, engage students in discussing the following questions:
  * *Did you say the same things as your partner about what makes you happy, sad, angry, scared or excited? Or were your responses different from your partner's?*
  * *Do people always have the same thoughts as you do?*
  * *Think of what your partner said that would make him/her happy, sad, mad, scared or excited. Would all of those same things make you just as happy, sad, mad, scared or excited? What if they're not the same as your partner's – what do you think that means about how powerful thought is?*

Discussion

Remember, our thoughts are so quick and go by so fast—faster than lightning—that sometimes we don't even know we're thinking them. Often, we just feel the feeling of them. That's how powerful thoughts are! Our thoughts create our feelings and our thoughts are what make us feel happy or sad or scared or excited at any given moment. In fact, our own thoughts are the only things that can make us feel anything. Nothing else can! We might think that what happens to us out in the world, like doing really well on a test (we feel good!) or a kid pushing us in line (we get angry), makes us have the feelings we do. But it's really the other way around. Our own thinking about it, how we see it in our minds, produces our feelings. For instance: when a kid pushes us in line, we might think, "Hey, he's being mean to me and now I'm angry!" or we could have a different thought, "He did that by accident, no big deal." Each of those two thoughts would produce a different feeling.

Lesson 3. Pages 6, 8.

Thought = Imagination

We can use our power of thought to imagine anything.

These illustrations show how thoughts also have another kind of power: the power to imagine anything. Everyone has thoughts. Most of the time our thoughts are different from everyone else's thoughts. Where do our thoughts come from? They come from us! Even though we don't realize we're making them up, they can't come from anyone else or anything else. Nobody knows why certain thoughts pop into our minds. Sometimes our thoughts are about what we see around us. But not always! Sometimes, we make up our thoughts, sort of like painting pictures in our minds about different things. That's our imagination! It comes from our own thoughts and we can use it to think up the most amazing things.

Some questions to ask and discuss with students:

❖ *What do you think the little guy is holding in his hand? (Point to illustration on page 6.)*

❖ *Did you notice that not everyone had the same thought about what he is holding? (A toy surfboard.) Why do you think that is?*

❖ *What do you think the little boy may be thinking about while playing with this toy surfboard? What do you think he might be imagining? (Turn to next page to find out.)*

❖ *Does the boy look like he's having fun, even though he's just pretending he's at the beach riding the waves? Look at how calm and cool he looks!*

Instruct students to imagine something they would like to be doing to have fun. After a few moments, invite students to describe what they imagined. As they take turns doing this, ask the group:

❖ *Can you imagine what the student is describing?*

❖ *How do you feel when you imagine yourself having fun?*

Discussion

See how powerful thoughts are? They can help you feel good even when you're not actually doing something fun. When you use your thought to imagine, you are doing the same thing the little guy in the picture is doing, except your own thoughts are giving you the feeling of happiness or excitement (or *whatever they came up with*). Whenever we want, we can imagine ourselves surfing or lying on a beach or (*mention what they came up with*), and those thoughts can make us feel nice. Thought can be used to make us feel good! It can also be used to make us feel bad. Which one is up to us if we learn to understand our thoughts.

Lesson 4. Pages 10, 12.

Calm Mind Thinking versus Upset Mind Thinking

These illustrations suggest we can engage in two kinds of thinking. The page 8 illustration shows that sometimes our thinking is calm and feels good, like riding a wave or soaking up the sun. Our best decisions and ideas come from that kind of thinking. The page 10 illustration shows that sometimes we have the opposite kind of thinking: anger or confusion. Some of the children here appear to be pushing and grabbing. The little guy up top is watching all this and does not know what to think about the whole situation — but he knows it doesn't feel good.

The focus here is on perspective taking. There are many ways to think about any situation, like the many colors in a prism. The boy could get angry because some of the kids aren't doing what they're supposed to be doing. He could get scared because they might start pushing and grabbing him next. Or, he could stay calm and ignore these feelings, which come from his thinking, and instead keep feeling good himself. He could want to do something to help. All are examples of different possibilities of thought, within the same situation. Most of these children waiting for ice cream do not appear to have a calm mind. Whether the little guy watching stays calm or gets riled up is up to him. His own thinking about the situation will determine how he feels and acts.

We are always in charge of how we choose to act, and it all comes from our own thinking. What do we do with the thoughts that come into our mind? We are in the position to believe them or not. When we're calm, we usually can trust our thinking. Calm thoughts make us feel good. But, if we trust and follow our thinking when we're upset, it usually will make things worse. The page 12 illustration shows what can happen in the same scene when everyone acts out of a calm place.

Listening to thoughts from a calm mind makes us feel and act better than listening to thoughts from an upset mind.

Activity. **The Glitter Jar** (appropriate for grades K-1)

Materials:

One clear container or jar with secure lid

Water

A few shakes of glitter (dark colors work best)*

1 Tbsp. corn syrup (to thicken water)

Tape

Handout: "The Glitter Jar"

* Note: As an alternative you could use mud in the water, but mud takes a long time to settle, while the glitter takes only a short time.

Instructions:

* Teacher makes a Glitter Jar (similar to a snow globe) ahead of time by filling the container with water, corn syrup and glitter. Secure lid on container with tape, as jar will be shaken repeatedly!

* Introduce the Glitter Jar to the class. Pass around for children to explore.

* Explain that the Glitter Jar represents our thinking. Ask children to think of a time they felt really calm or peaceful. As children describe their calm thoughts and feelings, hold the glitter jar very still, to let the glitter settle to the bottom.

* Ask children to describe a time they were really upset or mad. This time, vigorously shake the Glitter Jar to represent "mixed-up thinking." Ask children if they think it is a good time to act when they have mixed-up thinking.**

* Point out to the children that when the Glitter Jar is still, the mixed up stuff inside settles and clears on its own. Model a few deep breaths as you set the jar down to represent how we can help calm our bodies when we feel riled up. Discuss that our mind and our bodies eventually settle on their own, just like the glitter in the Glitter Jar settles, calms, and the water clears when it is not disturbed. Ask children if they think it would be a good time to act when their minds are calm and clear, compared with when they have mixed-up [or mud mind] thinking.

* Keep the Glitter Jar readily available for children to go to and shake as needed when they are feeling mixed up inside. The handout may be used as a visual reminder.

Calm Thinking   Mixed Up Thinking

** Note: If you do use mud, it is very illustrative to call this type of thinking "mud mind" as opposed to having a clear mind. You could still use that term if you tell the kids to imagine the glitter is mud.

Activity. **Exploring Calm versus Mixed Up Thought** (appropriate for grades 2-5)

Instructions:

❖ Point to the bottom of the page 10 illustration.

❖ Ask students what they think is happening with these kids waiting to buy ice cream; entertain ideas from students. When they are done, explain that your thinking tells you it looks like a couple of the kids are trying to push their way into the line, and one may be ready to fight.

❖ Probe students' thoughts about the situation:

- *How would you feel if someone pushed you in line?*

- *If you felt angry, what would you do? How would you act?*

- *If you felt afraid, what would you do? How would you act?*

- *If you felt (whatever else they said), what would you do? How would you act? Isn't it interesting that people would do different things just because they had different feelings?*

- *Do you remember where feelings come from? (From our own thinking.)*

❖ Direct attention to the little guy at the top of the page. Explain that he might be wondering about all this and that the prism represents the many different thoughts he may be having. He is stepping back with a calm mind, looking at the situation, and wondering, "What would I do if I was pushed in line?"

❖ Ask students questions about their thoughts and feelings (ie, their perspectives):

- *How would his feeling be different if his mind was calm, compared with if his mind was in the same state as the kids in line?*

- *What do you think he would do if his mind stayed calm?*

- *What do you think he would do if his mind was all mixed up or riled up?*

- *What do you think is the state of mind of the kids who are pushing and fighting?*

❖ Turn to page 12 and discuss this illustration, which is a similar situation:

- *What do you think is the kids' state of mind now?*

- *How do you think they're feeling?*

- *What do you think is the relationship between a calm mind and how those kids are feeling?*

- *Do you think it's possible for kids to get into trouble when they're calm?*

- *What do you think you might do when your mind isn't calm?*

- *What type of strategies could you use to regain calm or does your mind eventually calm on its own?*

Discussion

When we're feeling calm, we can trust what we're thinking. Those are the thoughts we can rely on. That's also when we're at our best and our best ideas come to us. When we're upset or angry or worried, our thoughts get all mixed up. When we feel this way it is wise to wait and regain calm before we act so we won't cause any harm and won't get into trouble. Strategies to regain calm include waiting a few minutes before saying or doing anything to let yourself calm down or taking a few deep breaths.

Sidebar to the Teacher of Children with Social Learning Challenges

Typical children come into this world with a social thinking brain that evolves along a developmental path, from more concrete to more nuanced understanding. This includes early social referencing skills such as joint attention ("Look, there's a rabbit in the front yard!") where children understand that others can point out helpful, important, or interesting information to us, to more sophisticated social skills such as being able to read nonverbal body language or pick up sarcasm or innuendo from others.

However, children with autism spectrum disorders and others with social thinking deficits may not have the same social "hard wiring" in their brain.

These children will miss some, many, or sometimes all of the social cues that as adults, we take for granted they understand. Being able to take the perspective of another person is one such skill. Hand in hand with perspective taking is the ability to empathize with the emotions of others. Often these children struggle to understand what people really mean by what they say and/or read body language and facial expressions, and at a more basic level, understand that people's thoughts differ from one another.

With younger children, our goal is to introduce perspective taking as it applies to the individual child. We encourage children to explore their own thoughts and feelings in relation to the world around them. With older children, we expand that awareness to include the thoughts and feelings of others. If students in your classroom exhibit difficulty understanding any of the preceding questions that require "putting yourself in someone else's shoes", we encourage you to learn more about perspective taking, including different levels of this skill within individuals, as described in detail in Michelle Garcia Winner's book, *Thinking About YOU Thinking About ME*. Also find helpful articles on her website, www.socialthinking.com.

**Find Lesson Plans and Activities
along with Handouts on the enclosed CD.**

What is a Thought?
(A Thought is a Lot)

Lesson Plan
&
Handouts

Social
Thinking.com

By
Jack Pransky and Amy Kahofer

©2012 Jack Pransky and Amy Kahofer.
Published by www.socialthinking.com

Social Thinking books, curriculum, and related products by Michelle Garcia Winner and Social Thinking Publishing

Core Books about the Social Thinking Model & Curriculum

Inside Out: What Makes a Person with Social Cognitive Deficits Tick?

Thinking About You Thinking About Me, 2nd Edition

Think Social! A Social Thinking Curriculum for School Age Students

Thinksheets for Teaching Social Thinking and Related Skills

*Social Behavior Mapping: Connecting Behavior,
Emotions and Consequences Across the Day* *

*Why Teach Social Thinking?
Questioning Our Assumptions About What It Means to Learn Social Skills*

For Early Learners

The Incredible Flexible You™ Storybooks and Curriculum for Early Learners
(co-authored with Ryan Hendrix, Kari Zweber Palmer & Nancy Tarshis)

The Incredible Flexible You™ Music CD Words and music by Tom Chapin & Phil Galdston

Whole Body Listening Larry at Home! By Kristen Wilson & Elizabeth Sautter

Whole Body Listening Larry at School! By Elizabeth Sautter & Kristen Wilson

*We Can Make it Better! A Strategy to Motivate and Engage Young Learners
in Social Problem-Solving Through Flexible Stories* By Elizabeth M. Delsandro

For School-Age Children

You Are a Social Detective! (co-authored by Pamela Crooke) **

Superflex... A Superhero Social Thinking Curriculum (co-authored by Stephanie Madrigal)

Superflex Takes on Glassman and the Team of Unthinkables (co-authored by Stephanie Madrigal)

Superflex Takes on Brain Eater and the Team of Unthinkables (co-authored by Stephanie Madrigal)

Superflex Takes on One-Sided Sid, Un-Wonderer and the Team of Unthinkables (co-authored by Stephanie Madrigal)

Sticker Strategies: Practical Strategies to Encourage Social Thinking and Organization, 2nd Edition

I Get It! Building Social Thinking and Reading Comprehension Through Book Chats By Audra Jensen, M.Ed., BCBA

The Zones of Regulation®: A Curriculum Designed to Foster Self-Regulation and Emotional Control By Leah M. Kuypers, MA Ed., OTR/L

*Available in English and Spanish **Available in English, French, and Spanish

Other Products

Thought Bubble (dry erase) Available in Blue or Green

Twin-Pack Speech Bubbles (dry erase)

Superflex Superdecks: (Card Game)

Thinkables & Unthinkables Double Deck

You are a Social Detective Interactive CD

Superflex Poster

The Zones of Regulation® Three Poster Set

Four Posters for the Classroom and Treatment Room

Visit our website for more information on our books and products, free articles on Social Thinking topics, and a listing of Social Thinking Conferences across the U.S.

www.socialthinking.com